The Asperger Love Guide

The Asperger Love Guide

A practical guide for adults with Asperger's syndrome to seeking, establishing and maintaining successful relationships

Genevieve Edmonds and Dean Worton

First published 2005
Reprinted 2007

Paul Chapman Publishing
A SAGE Publications Company
1 Oliver's Yard
55 City Road
London EC1Y 1SP

SAGE Publications Inc.
2455 Teller Road
Thousand Oaks, California 91320

SAGE Publications India Pvt Ltd.
B-42, Panchsheel Enclave
Post Box 4109
New Delhi 110 017

Commissioning Editor: Barbara Maines

Editorial Team: Mel Maines, Wendy Ogden, Sarah Lynch, Mike Gibbs

Designer: Jess Wright

A catalogue record for this book is available from the British Library

Library of Congress Control Number 2005907300

ISBN 978 1 4129 1910 4

Printed on paper from sustainable resources

Printed in Great Britain by The Cromwell Press Ltd, Trowbridge, Wiltshire

About the authors

Dean Worton is a 32 year old individual with Asperger's syndrome. He runs a successful UK-based website supporting adults with Asperger's syndrome in the UK and hosts real life meet-ups for its members. He also works in administration. He lives in north-west England.

Genevieve Edmonds is a 24 year individual with Asperger's syndrome. Genevieve speaks UK wide in the field of autism. Also within the field she writes, gives workshops, consultation and support for people 'disabled by society' in association with organisations such as The Missing link Support Services Ltd in north-west England. She lives and works in a solution-focused way.

Acknowledgements

Luke Beardon for your wonderful foreword and your great Asperger-friendly attitude. Andrew Bailey for your great photography. Also to Andrew and Mand for your excellent case-studies and to our publishers for recognising the need for this guide.

Thank you all.

Dedications

Genevieve

To my family for their ever-loving support throughout good and bad times in my life. Thankyou.

Also to Vicky Bliss, for the way you believe in people.

Dean

To my family for their care and support and also to my cousin Julie who gave me so much invaluable support without which this book may never have been possible.

Contents

Foreword

Asperger's syndrome (and autism) have played a major part for over a third of my life now, and the more I work within the field the more I realize that I know less than I thought! I feel a deep sense of privilege to be working in such a complex, enjoyable, fascinating, frustrating, absorbing field full of so many charismatic individuals, and I am further indebted to people like Gen and Dean who have done so much to help me and other 'NTs' understand them. Although I currently hold an 'academic' title and work for a university, I am of the opinion that the majority of my learning and understanding people with AS has stemmed directly from individuals themselves – either from direct contact or through writing. It is with great pleasure, therefore, that I am able to introduce a new text written by people with AS who demonstrate an aptitude for presenting a difficult subject area in such an accessible manner.

Relationships can be a headache for many people. For individuals with AS the problems are often multiplied to an unmanageable degree. Many people with AS that I know remark on the difficulties they have had in trying to understand how best to get into a relationship, or how to hold onto one. Yet so many of these same individuals also comment that a relationship is something that they strive for and is of paramount importance. Thus, it seems clear that there is a large group of individuals who have a distinct need in a complex area, but with very little in terms of support. There is a definite lack of literature available to assist people with AS in understanding the nature of relationships and how to go about developing and maintaining one. This is in contrast with the wealth of literature available for neurotypical people – just one of a multitude of examples of how poorly recognized, understood, and supported the needs of people with AS are. It is the duty of a just society to ensure that with the passage of time these needs are met, and from the perspective of people with AS and their families, the sooner the better. With written accounts by people with AS becoming more widely published the platform upon which to build better and more appropriate support services will grow stronger. It is then down to the neurotypical population to learn from the growing literature, and to use that platform to provide that support as and when it is needed.

There is nothing, absolutely nothing, inherently wrong with having AS. Repeat until convinced! I abhor the notion that just because someone is different, behaves in a different way, or has 'non typical' characteristics, then that individual is in some way automatically considered to be lesser than their NT peer group. And yet people with AS are disadvantaged in a multitude of ways every day just for having AS. Rather than celebrating the richness and depth of character that many people with AS have, rather than learning from the unique way in which individuals with AS think and process information, rather than ensuring that people with AS are supported to live their lives to their fullest potential as they deserve, far too often people with AS are misunderstood and marginalised and made to feel worthless, simply because they think in a different way. Yet where would we be without difference? I believe that the world would be a very different place without AS – and not for the better. People with AS provide society with challenges, certainly. However, the reaction of society to somehow blame the individual with AS (directly or indirectly) rather than shouldering the responsibility of the challenges – and meeting them in a supportive capacity – seems inadequate at the least, unethical and unlawful at worst.

The concept that having AS is just both positive and negative, is finally filtering through the literature. This is because people with AS refuse to accept that the only way forward is to become less Asperger and celebrating the fact that they have AS. This places considerable responsibility on society to develop an understanding of AS in a global sense and to change perspectives and challenge perceptions. This is a responsibility that all people who want equality and anti-discriminatory practice to exist should take forward, promote, and act upon. With the help of people with AS this is a realistic and achievable goal, and one which all professionals in the field of autism and AS could be and should be striving towards.

There are several autobiographical accounts written by people with AS that offer a superb insight into the way in which that particular individual thinks and experiences the world. There are fewer texts written by individuals offering their views and advice for other people with AS. What Gen and Dean have done in *The Asperger Love Guide* is combine their own unique experiences, link it with their understanding of AS, and produced a book invaluable to other people with AS. This is not to say that you need to have AS to read it and gain something from it. In fact I would encourage anyone who has any contact with a person with AS to read this and to learn from it. The text is very easy to read and provides the reader with excellent advice and information on one of the most complex subjects in society – certainly one of the most problematic areas for individuals with AS themselves. Gen and Dean have managed to take a highly charged and difficult subject and provide an extremely readable and sensible book on the subject, for which they deserve congratulations and thanks.

Luke Beardon
Senior Lecturer in Autism Sheffield Hallam University

Introduction

So you're an adult with a diagnosis of Asperger's syndrome, or you may suspect that you have Asperger's syndrome. You may have been told that AS is a disorder of social communication, interaction, imagination and hence a deficit in the ability to form and maintain relationships, especially romantic relationships. You may know this from your own experience, you may feel that everyone else seems to have successful relationships and can't work out why not you? You may feel that you would be capable of having a relationship, but just don't know how to go about it. If any of this sounds familiar, this guide is for you. This guide aims to dispel the myth that adults with AS cannot or will always struggle to have successful relationships in adulthood. The guide aims to empower AS adults with the knowledge and skills to get on the way to having happy and successful relationships.

The guide does not make distinctions in culture, sexuality, race, gender, social class and so on. It is written from the point of view of a heterosexual relationship as this is from our own personal experience. However, the tips and strategies are aimed at a relationship non-specific to any of the differentiations as outlined. It is designed to be written in the style of a 'friend to a friend' from the AS point of view. We are not psychologists or relationship experts. The advice given in the book is aimed as self-help support to other Aspies, but is not guaranteed to give 100% success. It does, however, aim to help fellow adult Aspies on their way to successful love lives.

It is not an academic critique of Asperger's syndrome and relationships, nor an autobiographical or biographical account of AS and relationships. There are many of these books around. This is a practical guide that you can pick up and use written by two people who have insight into how life may be for you as an individual with AS. We all may have AS but we are still people and not here just for the purposes of stories and academic or scientific study but to have real everyday lives like everyone else!

NB There are no official rules in the dating game – they are a matter of opinion and may be affected by a number of personal, cultural and social factors. We have tried to keep this as general as possible to appeal to a wide audience.

The merits of the single life

Many people on the autistic spectrum really want to be in a romantic relationship; however, there are others who are happy to remain celibate and single, or have non-sexual relationships. This can change throughout life and is not static. The key is to do what makes you happy as an individual and to be sure that you make a choice to be in a relationship for the right reasons. Wrong reasons for being in a relationship are due to pressures of society not to be single, as a means of fitting in or just because 'everyone else seems to be with someone.' Being single or celibate can be just as rewarding as a relationship. The single life can allow a person to concentrate on areas of their life, which may be of more importance to them such as their career, their work, their family or their interests. There are no right and wrong answers to the relationship question. You will know what is right for you. Counselling with a therapist who understands AS can be helpful to clarify what you want out of life. (See Useful Contacts.)

Terminology used in this guide

Aspie – The target group for the guide. This refers to an able, high functioning adult with Asperger's syndrome, however, the book can be used for lower functioning adults on the autistic spectrum with support from a support worker, carer or trusted friend.

NTs – a term used for the purposes of writing referring to mainstream neurologically 'normal' (neurotypical) individuals.

AS – Asperger's syndrome.

Partner – a general term used for the purpose of writing for boyfriend, girlfriend or mate and to avoid cultural, sexuality, racial, regional, gender and related differences.

ASD – Autistic Spectrum Disorder.

Stims – self-stimulatory behaviour: repetitive motor or vocal mannerisms engaged in by people with ASDs. They are usually used to either calm or excite the nervous system and often as a response to strong emotion.

Chapter 1

Asperger's Syndrome and Relationships: The Reality

The science bit

Aspies are seen to view the world in a logical, scientific and intellectual way rather than an innate way. Following on from this concept, to begin with we thought we would add in a section on the science behind relationships.

According to scientific theory the process of attraction and love is based on our own biochemistry. What determines who we are attracted to is subconscious. It is based on our genetic make-up. The theory goes that when we fancy someone, it is actually because our mind is subconsciously attracted to their genetic make-up.

Scientists believe that certain brain chemicals which are given out at different stages of the love process drive the stages of attraction we go through. Initially we fall in lust (a deep physical attraction based on sexual hormones) then a deep attraction occurs which relates to falling in love with the whole person, mind and body. The chemicals produced at this stage of attraction are the ones, which cause us to feel those 'lovey-dovey' feelings such as being 'lovesick', or 'madly in love.' Finally we may enter a stage where we become attached to someone and want to make a commitment. The couple may then bond and the chemicals produced here serve to keep the couple together for producing and bringing up children.

Other theories are that we are subconsciously attracted to people that resemble ourselves and that we are drawn to people who have similar facial and bodily features.

Some psychologists believe that without being aware of it we look for mates who are actually like our own parents in appearance and personality, again pointing to a compatible genetic make-up. Hence, men look for women like their mothers, and women, like their fathers. Who would think it?!

Of course in the real world if it were this simple we wouldn't be writing this guide. Beyond science is the social world that also determines our relations with others. For Aspies, the social world is the tough part of relating to others, so read on for help with this!

The way of the world

People with ASDs make up a minority of the population, so the other 90+% of folks determine the status quo. Some of this majority judge everything people do but wait, isn't it a free country? The simple answer is YES; you can do or be anything you want as long as you're not hurting yourself or anyone else (within reason and of course not breaking the law!).

Perhaps you make your own clothes, ride a bike everywhere, drink hot chocolate on a night out and don't support a football team. Well, good for you!

The first type of person might prefer:

● designer clothes

● flash cars

● binge drinking culture

● watching football.

The other type of person may prefer:

● buying or making cheap clothes

● going nowhere without your bicycle

● drinking hot chocolate in a pub at night

● playing chess.

Many people wrongly believe that everyone ought to be the first type of person and treat the other group as outcasts. Yet, the second group has every right to do their preferred activities and should be proud to be individuals. If anything, their activities are safer and they may make more interesting people. If you are more likely to belong to the second group then good for you!

It is a free country after all and thank goodness that some people don't follow the crowd because the world would be very dull if no one was individual.

There is no right or wrong way to be and no one has the right to judge us. If anyone has a problem with you, more often than not it is that person with the problem and not you.

Perceived problems

We're now going to tell you something that may completely shock you. A lot of the things that you may see as a barrier to relationships are not. They are either based on someone else's exaggeration or you being too hard on yourself. People with AS often have a negative opinion of themselves because other people's harsh comments make them feel like they are poor human beings. We're going to surprise you by telling you no matter how pathetic you have been made to feel by others you actually have as many good qualities and maybe more.

It's likely that some of these people delight in putting other people down to cover up their own shortcomings. Possible things that are perceived as problems but aren't necessarily may include:

● strange mannerisms

● interests perceived as boring or nerdy

● strange walking style

● flat, monotonous voice

● strange choice of clothes

● lack of social confidence.

The people who put others down because of these things need to learn a thing or two about empathy. These people could be less likely to make a good partner themselves. The good news is that there are plenty of people who will accept you as you are. In fact, many people may be relieved to find such a nice, polite, caring person. Some may consider you to be a rare find that they don't want to lose. After all people with AS can be quite fascinating.

The reality of Asperger's syndrome and relationships

Relationships can be very complex for most people and are not something to be taken lightly, and everyone has to work hard at relationships. The results are often very rewarding, but as an individual with AS, you will need to develop empathy and understanding towards the other person. This can be difficult for anyone, but is often harder for people with Asperger's syndrome due to the different way our mind works. We might find it more difficult to be aware of the various ways in which our partner may expect or assume we should or will interact. In a world where NTs often find it hard to meet people and have trouble with relationships, it can be much more difficult for people with AS to meet people to have a relationship with! Although it may seem like everyone around you has a successful relationship, it is not always the case, and even when it is the case it is hard!

Many Aspies simply start the relationship process later rather then not at all. Many Aspies have their first relationship long after their teens and some much later. Some maybe, as yet, would say their relationship history is nil. It is fully possible to learn to navigate the social world intellectually rather than innately, as NTs would. Many Aspies become remarkably skilled at this, and can mask their difficulties so well that it is often hard to tell that they have a diagnosis of AS. AS is not static. With support Aspies can improve their understanding of how the social world works and the accompanying rules. We are both examples of this. Both of us have improved in leaps and bounds with our AS since we both separately (before we knew each other) chose to learn and to work with our AS and not against it. Nowadays we have control over our own individual presentation of AS. The difficult and negative aspects of AS can be overcome, so that what is left are the many wonderful gifts that AS can bring.

Well, you know the reality, so please do take heart. We absolutely believe that with the right learning, support and understanding of AS in a relationship scenario Aspies can have happy and successful relationships. If you have picked up this guide in the first place, you have already made a sensible first step. By the end of reading it, you will be many, many positive steps closer towards your own relationship goals.

Autism and emotion

One of the main problems with the way autistic individuals are seen by non-autistic individuals is that their autistic behaviour is often associated with emotion. Let us give you two examples:

1. You have sensory defensiveness. Hugging can be quite uncomfortable for you. This is not associated with your feelings towards the person hugging you; it is to do with your different mind. The non-autistic person assumes you have negative emotions towards them because you don't like being hugged by them. They take offence, this ruins the relationship.

2. You get easily overloaded by listening, talking, making eye contact and interacting over long periods. You need time alone to rebalance and re-energize yourself to interact further. The non-autistic person assumes that when you go off a lot to be on your own that you dislike their company and that you are rude. This of course is not true; this is difficult for the relationship.

As far as is known, autism is not an emotionally determined condition. It can be associated with emotions, but it is not emotions that cause it. This is essential knowledge to have for your relationships. Without this knowledge between you and your partner your relationship could suffer. We explore the effects of AS on relationships in the following table.

AS Characteristics	Possible Outcome	Managing Outcome
Discomfort with physical affection.	Partner may think you are cold and might feel that you have lost interest in them emotionally.	Explain that AS can make affection uncomfortable for you due to sensory defensiveness. Partner could learn to show affection in a less intense and intrusive way.
Frequent anger/frustration.	Could frighten partner or they may find your reactions irrational, out of proportion or abnormal.	Explain to partner what makes you react that way and how frustrating and tough life can be with AS. Bear in mind, however, that life is frustrating for everyone and you could control your reaction to some extent.
High levels of anxiety.	Anxiety can be a barrier in a relationship and cause problems if it makes it impossible or difficult for you to do something, which your partner wants you both to do.	Learn that anxiety is a natural part of AS; don't give yourself a hard time over it. Work with it by channelling excess anxiety into positive tasks. Accept that often you could be anxious about nothing.

AS Characteristics	Possible Outcome	Managing Outcome
Difficulties with eye contact.	Your partner could find your lack of, over intense eye contact or 'odd' eye contact off-putting.	Look at their mouth or nose to give the impression of appropriate eye contact. Ask them to allow you times without eye contact. Learn together about appropriate eye contact.
Resistance to change.	Could make the relationship stale or 'stuck in a rut'.	Accept that change is a healthy and natural part of life. If possible deal with new situations gradually, or step-by-step.
Over-dependency.	Could make your partner feel trapped, feel they are a mother figure.	Learn to be able to do things, that due to your AS, you find hard of your own accord. Ask for support or written instructions initially.
Depression.	May make it hard for your partner to connect with you, they may blame themselves.	Seek medical help. Depression is easily treatable with medication and counselling. It is very common with AS. Try to understand your partner's fears, talk about your own. Think of all the nice things people have said and done for you.

AS Characteristics	Possible Outcome	Managing Outcome
Over-sensitivity.	This could make your partner feel that they have to be very careful about everything they say or do.	Your past AS traumas may have caused you to become over-sensitive. Be aware that you both may have to accept that you are sensitive and accept that your partner may not be trying to upset or offend you.
Lies.	You may be ashamed of the way your AS affects your life and consequently lie to cover it up. This breaks essential trust.	Always be truthful with each other from the beginning. If lies have already been told you need to get everything out in the open and talk things through for the health of your relationship.
Food sensitivities.	Could be frustrating when preparing meals to eat together. Could appear like faddy or indulgent behaviour.	Accept together that those with AS may be over-sensitive to certain foods. Always be prepared, however, to try new things. If you can't stand the new food, at least you've tried. Try to meet each other halfway in joint meal preparation.

AS Characteristics	Possible Outcome	Managing Outcome
Self-absorption.	Partner will find it hard to connect with you and feel shut out.	Accept that AS can make you appear egocentric. This is not always true; you may need space to re-energize or to feel less overloaded. Explain that this is not related to your love for them. Involve your partner in as much as you can cope with.
Lack of care with appearance.	You may appear odd, sloppy, or lazy.	Aspies can forget the importance of the social priority of a neat and tidy appearance. Ask your partner for help in maintaining a decent appearance.
Attachment to objects.	This can appear odd or self-indulgent if you constantly need to have certain objects near you.	Allow your partner to learn that having certain objects near can help to relieve anxieties for you. Explain the importance of feeling confused and stressed, for example, if you have to carry your phone/ watch/ timetable at all times if these are important to you.

AS Characteristics	Possible Outcome	Managing Outcome
Short attention span.	A short attention span may make you appear you have lost interest in your partner despite being able to pay attention for long periods on a social interest.	Make your partner aware that it is easy to excessively focus on a factual interest, but emotional or physical activities may make you become quickly overloaded. Try to compromise by keeping contact short but frequent between you.
Embarrassing, socially inappropriate or immature behaviour.	This may make your partner feel that they are being shown up.	Try to always think of the impact of your behaviour on those around you. If you struggle to understand socially appropriate or age appropriate behaviour, always consult your partner on how to behave. Always show willingness to learn.

AS Characteristics	Possible Outcome	Managing Outcome
Problems with keeping or finding appropriate employment.	Your partner may feel that they take too much financial responsibility, or may feel anger that you are under-employed for your abilities or qualifications.	Seek Asperger-appropriate employment. Consult AS employment support services/ web resources/ books. Always inform potential employers of your AS to avoid misunderstandings. Inform them of the positive points in employing someone with AS.
Failure.	If you convince yourself that you are a failure you are sealing your own fate. You will frustrate a caring and supportive partner.	Stop focusing on the negatives, concentrate on what you've done well in the past. Accept compliments and support from your partner.

AS Characteristics	Possible Outcome	Managing Outcome
Fears.	Your fears may appear out of proportion or nonsensical. This could alarm or anger your partner.	Accept support from your partner to alleviate your fears. Understand that having AS can make the world appear a frightening and bewildering place, make sure that your partner realizes this. Remember that your worst fears rarely occur at full effect.
Lack of awareness of dangers.	Can make your partner feel anxious and that they must 'mother' you.	Read safety guides and explain that AS can cause a lack of social understanding, for example, with danger. Ask for support if you need it, don't be ashamed to do this.
Attitudes to disability or 'difference'.	Negative attitudes from either you or your partner about AS will make the relationship negative.	Look at the positive aspects of your character together and learn to appreciate how wonderful you are. Accept together that AS is a 'difference' and becomes a 'disability' through its negative treatment by society.

AS Characteristics	Possible Outcome	Managing Outcome
Lack of friends or intrusive friendships.	Lack of friends may be a problem if your partner does have friends and may make things uncomfortable and unequal. The Aspie may resent the partner's friends or vice versa. Some friendships may intrude on a relationship, however, ignoring them may cause you or your partner to lose them.	Make time for each other's friends, respect both of your needs, even if different within friendship. Accept that friends are healthy even for a person with AS. Teach your partner that if your AS means that you don't need friends that this is healthy too. Accept that friends are like plants and need watering so they don't wilt away.
Difficulty reading non-verbal language.	Could be confusing for both you and your partner if you both struggle to read each other's non-verbal gestures.	Understand that non-verbal language is hard for those with AS to read and use. Ask for explanation for clarity over what each of your non-verbal language means.
Stims.	Your partner may feel your stims are odd and may not accept or empathize with your need to stim.	Try to reduce stims around your partner if they upset them. Stim only in appropriate agreed places. Explain why you need to perform stims.

AS Characteristics	Possible Outcome	Managing Outcome
Incompatibility with frequency of touch.	Too much or too little touch between you or your partner could be wrongly associated with emotion.	Explain that your lack of touch is not due to your feelings but that you have sensory discomfort with touch at times. Touching too much could be related to not understanding your partner's needs through their non-verbal language. Discuss a compromise.
Hyperactivity.	Can be difficult for your partner to be around you when you are hyperactive, it can be exhausting.	Try to identify situations where it is appropriate to remain calm and still. If you cannot control your hyperactivity seek medical advice.
Over-independence.	Being too independent could be perceived as creating deliberate distance within the relationship.	If you need independence more than your partner, make them feel more involved when you are together.

AS Characteristics	Possible Outcome	Managing Outcome
Unusual intelligence.	Could make basic communication and general conversation difficult if unable to separate intellectualizing from everyday life.	Don't talk excessively about intellectual topics and don't show off your knowledge any more than you have to. Those with AS intellectualize the world in order to understand a world they innately don't. Accept that this is a requirement for coping in life as an Aspie.
Logical approach to relationships.	The use of logic rather than empathy and emotion to approach relationships can appear cold, uncaring or callous.	Explain to your partner that a strength of the AS individual can be the ability to separate emotion from logic and can be helpful in relationships. Explain how much you love them and that your logical approach does not reflect your feelings for or your empathy towards them. If you need help with empathy ask for it from a counselor or partner.

AS Characteristics	Possible Outcome	Managing Outcome
Obsessive compulsive behaviour; rituals and routines.	Your partner may perceive obsessive compulsive behaviour, following apparently inconsequential routines and rituals, as a waste of time, impinging on the relationship, odd or unhealthy.	Explain why you find your behaviour difficult to change, that it helps you to make sense of a very confusing and frightening world and the anxiety that comes with it. If your routines, rituals or obsessive compulsive behaviour is out of control and seriously affecting your relationship, seek help from an AS qualified psychotherapist.
Lack of appropriate self-care.	Your partner may feel responsible for you and may resent having to constantly help you to appropriately care for yourself.	Understand that lack of social understanding can cause you to omit seemingly obvious aspects of self-care. Draw up checklists together to ensure that self-care is kept up without prompting from your partner.

AS Characteristics	Possible Outcome	Managing Outcome
Difficulty with space.	Lack of awareness of appropriate personal space can cause annoyance and distress to a partner.	If you constantly invade your partner's space or distance yourself too much your partner can take it personally. Each of you has a right to your own space, but equally need to be close too. Try to learn appropriate space rules.
Difficulty with awareness of passage of time.	This can make everyday life very disordered.	Seek support from your partner in developing strategies to become more aware of time. Accept that those on the autistic spectrum struggle with the concept of time and try to work with your strengths to help with this.
Trouble getting out and about.	Can restrict the relationship and stifle each other.	Take appropriate medication to alleviate anxiety, learn relaxation and breathing techniques. Talk to an AS trained psychotherapist for support.

Aspie-Aspie relationships

Aspies come in different shapes and sizes and differ as much from each other as NTs do. For example, an NT could be shy just as easily as an Aspie could be extrovert. However, we all have one thing in common: we find it very difficult to fit in with the world.

This may mean that the other person understands how we feel and doesn't think we are weird or a moaner. We can be supportive and patient towards each other. The other person is possibly more likely to understand our different thinking style and off the wall humour and who knows they might share it with you. We may already have an innate understanding of the psychology of our partner as we can identify similarities in our Aspergian behaviour to ourselves. It may be easier to find a soulmate more quickly as we are both 'aliens' in the world.

The typical AS stereotype of a completely socially disabled, odd individual who may be totally obsessed with a special interest or someone completely lacking in empathy seems to now be a bit outdated. This may be due to the fact that AS is now more frequently diagnosed and hence, the stereotype was probably borne out of more severe cases who would have been noticed when the rest of us with AS wouldn't. We have both met many adults with AS and although we all share the same type of 'brain wiring' we all have individual characters and personalities.

Chapter 2

You

There is more than a bit of truth in the saying 'You can't love another until you love yourself'.

This chapter aims to sort out 'you' before you embark on dating or a relationship. As you may be aware, or may discover, being secure and happy in yourself is fundamental before you consider a relationship.

Acceptance of your AS and the reality of having AS

If you have a diagnosis of Asperger's syndrome, or you are self-diagnosed, then reaching a state of acceptance of your condition is essential before you embark on a close relationship with another. Having AS certainly does not have to be a negative thing, but being aware of how your AS affects you individually and in the wider world is important. Many Aspies describe often feeling like an 'alien' or 'another species'. There is no doubt that AS can, and does, affect how a person understands the world around them and how they approach life. Often accepting you have AS can be likened to a 'grieving' process. In some ways accepting that you have a different neurological make-up can be like bereavement. You have perhaps lost the person you thought you were, or the picture of 'normality' that you hoped to fulfil in your life. For many, diagnosis is a relief and a happy time. Diagnosis allows for understanding of yourself and the opportunity to gain support and sometimes to feel at long last a sense of belonging.

When translating all of this into a potential relationship situation, it makes sense that acceptance of yourself is better dealt with before embarking on forming a partnership with someone else. Acceptance of your AS involves having a medical diagnosis, especially one such as AS which is lifelong; the shedding of an old identity or perhaps some hopes you had; and coming to terms with having a new understanding of yourself and what lies ahead. All of these things take time and emotional and physical energy. Once you have got the process of acceptance out of the way, you can give all of your energy to forming a new relationship. See Chapter 3 for details about disclosing your AS.

Get to know yourself

Often in relationships one or both halves of the relationship decide to break it off in search of 'themselves'. Simply translated, this is a stage that takes place in everyone's life when they need to discover who they are (that is, their true personality, beliefs, dreams, morals and so on) and what they hope to get out of their life. This is an ongoing process, but it is much easier to get to know yourself without having to cope with the responsibilities that come with a relationship. Trying to get to know yourself first also avoids the possibility of a relationship breaking up when you then discover where your life is going.

You need to know and understand yourself if your partner is going to get to know you. Otherwise this could cause problems and misunderstanding if your actions or lack of them could be misinterpreted as something which was not intentional. You shouldn't analyze yourself too much either. There isn't a single person alive who has no good points and you can turn every negative opinion of yourself into a positive one. Most people with AS have many, many wonderful traits so you should rejoice in that fact and not dwell on what you are not good at.

If you don't feel you have got to know yourself well yet, do not try to measure yourself by NT standards or the characteristics that the world at large may expect. Try to educate yourself about AS and how it affects you. Read as many AS biographies as you can get your hands on; chat with other Aspies online; talk to well-informed AS counsellors or therapists; talk to those close to you who have a good understanding of you. All of these things will help you to get to know yourself.

Self-esteem

This is all-important before you consider embarking on a relationship. It is pretty common for adult Aspies to be experiencing low self-esteem especially if they have had a late diagnosis. In adolescence and childhood they may have been blamed for their behaviour or told to try harder or that they were disturbed and so on. Low self-esteem for Aspies in adulthood can also occur due to the full realization of not fitting in and being different. The society we live in can be cruel to anyone in a minority or who is different, so with all the past trauma that may have occurred, coupled with realizing the extent of your AS, you may have to try hard initially to gain self-esteem. The first hurdle is the hardest – once you begin to accept and love yourself the way you are the rest will come naturally and you will build on your confidence without even trying. The longer you allow low esteem to grow the quicker your mental health will suffer and sadly depression, anxiety and even more serious mental illness could occur.

Low self-esteem can be caused by:

- always being told you were not good enough, odd, strange, weird
- bullying (emotional or physical), ostracism, humiliation
- not fitting in with peers, family or work colleagues

- blaming yourself for your differences
- not understanding 'why' you are different – no clear diagnosis
- wrong diagnoses by professionals, such as 'learning disabled', 'mentally ill' or 'self-inflicted behaviour'
- incorrect and unhelpful labels by others such as teachers, family, work colleagues or peers as 'lazy', 'unwilling', 'wilful', 'naughty', 'useless' and so on
- being a constant disappointment to others despite trying very hard
- setting perfectionist or unrealistically high standard for yourself
- many, many more things.

Signs of low self-esteem are:

- excessive shyness
- passive behaviour
- feeling inferior
- conforming when not wishing to
- apologizing for yourself constantly
- fear of failure and competition
- not accepting compliments
- allowing bad behaviour in others towards you
- fear of being rejected
- finding negativity and faults in others
- feeling constantly guilty or defensive
- being possessive or jealous.

Self-esteem boosting tips for Aspies

Aspies often:

- have a strong sense of social justice
- are straightforward, honest not game players

- place less emphasis on fashions, trends, appearance
- are thoughtful, intelligent
- have a very helpful ability to separate emotion from logic
- are accepting of those from all backgrounds.

Now build that self-esteem!

Some strategies are:

- realize that you are a good, special, unique and decent person
- discover that society's expectation for everyone to conform is unrealistic and unhealthy
- believe that those with AS actually do no more wrong that those without AS!
- accept your difference and stand up for your basic human rights to be yourself
- become a strong, assertive individual.

Positive thinking

There is nothing more attractive to others than a positive person. They exude sex appeal! Being around someone who tries to see the positive side of things is a joy. People will want to be around you more when you can try and do this. Difficult as it can be to accept we can tell you from our own experience that the phrase 'laugh and the world laughs with you, cry and you cry alone' is all too true. Most people will be sympathetic to a point but after a while constant negativity and hopelessness just pushes people away as they feel too inadequate to help you. Often the 'positive thinking' idea is seen as a load of rubbish, that it is self-deceit if you don't really believe it. However, it is more the act of being optimistic than the truth itself in what you believe to be positive which is beneficial. For Aspies, being positive, like building self-esteem, can be an uphill struggle but it is worth it. Your positivity may attract someone who can support you when you really can't be positive, but you may never attract someone until you make the first steps to being optimistic.

Change and improvement

To love someone you should never change them is what is often said
in relationship talk. However, it is OK to identify things you would like
to improve about yourself, this is a healthy way to be. Autism can be a
powerful ruler in that it is often very hard to alter your autistic behaviour
no matter how hard you try. However, with the right support (contacts can
be found in the back of this guide) such as counselling/ psychotherapy
and social skills practice some of your, perhaps, more problematic autistic
traits can be overcome, or at least improved. Improving and overcoming
behaviours that have been a part of you for a long time can be a very long
and difficult process. However, if you really want to build and maintain
a happy, successful relationship the hard work can be worth the effort.
Everyone has parts of their personality that need to be improved or altered
in a relationship situation. This is inevitable when you are spending a lot of
time with another person.

Individuality: being yourself

One of the great things about those with AS is their capability to be
individual. Many Aspies don't feel the need to follow the crowd. This
is a lovely trait to have. Celebrate your individuality. If you haven't yet
discovered it – do! An important factor in being one half of a relationship
is to know yourself and be happy with who you are as an individual. It is
very important to maintain your individuality in a relationship as well as the
things you equally share with your partner.

One of the reasons for depression and low self-esteem in some Aspies and
some NTs is that the world seems to operate on a series of expectations on
how we should live our lives. Life should not all be about competing with
each other, though sadly it often is. There is no need for you to go along
with this way of life; it is not a healthy sort of existence. Sometimes to
conform you could be expected to behave in ways which are not natural to
you, or your own sense of self or your beliefs. A consequence may be even
sometimes becoming vulnerable to criminal activity either as a perpetrator
or a victim. Having self-esteem gives you the strength of character to stay
away from influences you are uncomfortable with. You have every right to
be who you are.

As an Aspie you could have amazing knowledge and interest in one specific
topic. Why not embrace this and join a club where you can meet others like

you? If there is nothing suitable locally, why not join a web-group related to your interest, which may be full of like-minded people. Many Aspies seem to have strong, sometimes unusual interests and by joining such a group you may find for the first time an array of other individuals just like you!

Another great thing to do is to join Asperger web-groups to share your self-knowledge and individuality with others who would be appreciative of it and may help you to keep on the right track for you. Dean runs one such web-group entitled 'Aspie Village UK'. Details of this group are included at the back of the guide.

Don't ever try to be someone you're not, it is the worst thing you can do. You'll only be able to keep up the act for so long, and when the mask slips you'll have made a fool of yourself. Not being you and then being found out is a killer for relationships. Most people want to meet a nice, down-to earth, straightforward person and so what if you have a couple of faults? Nobody is perfect! Everyone has good qualities and someone out there will love you for yours, even if you have to be patient in waiting to meet them. It may seem harder because as an Aspie you are not 'mainstream' or like everyone else, when the right person comes along they will be the one who loves and appreciates your individuality and rarity.

Take responsibility

You are you. Unique, nobody in the world is the same as you. Sometimes Aspies get lumped together as though they are all the same just because they share the same diagnosis. This of course is not true. Each Aspie naturally has their own personality and life experiences. Therefore, always take responsibility for yourself. This is fundamental. Having a diagnosis or condition is never an excuse. Always strive to work hard with your strengths and recognize your weaknesses. If you can't overcome your weaknesses, try hard to work with them to make them easier for you and others to live with.

You need always to take responsibility for yourself if you are to have a successful relationship. You need to be aware of issues of personal safety and the safety of your partner. While always trying to have fun, there are situations which you need to take seriously, and you need to act appropriately at these times. Examples of these times could be personal safety while out and about such as ensuring your partner gets safely home, avoid being in areas where crime is common, observing drug laws, observing the law in general or engaging in safe sex.

Interests

One thing Aspies seem to often have in common is their ability to devotedly follow special interests. Some interests can be perceived by society as odd or weird and not conforming to the accepted norm.

If your interest does not damage yourself or others then by all means pursue it. Talking to someone who has a passion for something is very enjoyable. In a relationship sharing special interests can enhance it, but it is still important to continue to follow you own interest if this is important to you.

Another trait many Aspies have is to talk on and on without awareness of the listener being bored or uncomfortable and talking at the listener and not with them. This is perhaps due to:

- an absolute passion for a certain interest which reflects in lengthy monologues as the speaker may be enthusiastic they have so much to say

- being unaware of the social rules of interaction which state that unless a speaker is supposed to be lecturing someone, such as at a conference or university, the speaker is expected to allow the listener to also speak and join in

- being unaware of non-verbal signals such as facial expression, body language and eye contact, which show the person is uncomfortable or bored.

As you may have guessed, going and on and on in monologues to someone about your interest is generally seen as rude and a turn-off. Unless the listener is as keen as you are about your subject, the safest option is to talk in short bursts about the subject, asking if the listener wants to hear more and asking their opinion about what you are saying. Then you can't be accused of talking 'at' someone as you will be speaking 'with them'.

As many Aspies do have strong and intense interests, it may be worth seeking a partner in places where your interest can be pursued. Sharing a similar passionate interest can certainly help the formation of a relationship as well as keeping one, as you have something guaranteed in common.

Emotional baggage

Everyone carries emotional baggage which is unresolved past emotions or traumas. This is inevitable. If you have lived with either diagnosed or undiagnosed AS to adulthood there is a fair chance that you will have some trauma behind you. This could be having been bullied, excluded or made to feel inadequate, odd or alien. Some are lucky enough not to, but if you have had some emotional trauma in your life of any sort you may be carrying some emotional baggage. A nice thing in a relationship is that trauma can be worked through together and each of you can support each other to deal with it. However, this is something that is really only suitable when you have reached a more intense stage of the relationship.

Being Aspie, a good part of your life may have been emotionally tough and you may be carrying more of this baggage around with you than you realize. A mistake that can be made when in a new relationship, or even when dating, can be to reveal too much of your baggage too soon. This is easily understood if it has featured a lot in your life, but in a new or growing relationship, it is best to stay as neutral and as positive as possible. Too much emotional intensity can scare people away or can make the person appear too dependent too soon.

Appearance

Aspies are notoriously known as having a less than average interest in their personal appearance. It has been said that Aspies have poor personal hygiene, poor fashion sense and odd clothing choices. Make of this what you will, it could be perceived as perhaps that many Aspies are too busy thinking about more important things than to worry too much about their looks! Maybe it's that many Aspies place more importance on what is inside than on the outside, who knows? Some Aspies are not followers of trends or fashion. Such people may like to create their own fashion reflecting their individuality. Others couldn't care even as much as that and will put on any old thing. A fact of life is that the majority of the world, DO place much emphasis on personal hygiene, appropriate dress and fashion. I think a compromise is the safest option for an Aspie to take here. When entering the dating game, making an effort with one's appearance is perceived as an absolute must. Not doing so is perceived as odd or rude social behaviour.

The best thing to do is to consult a trusted person who has a good understanding of appropriate appearance rules in mainstream society.

If your wardrobe is severely lacking, ask them to take you shopping to purchase suitable outfits for such occasions. Sorry to say it, but where you go also affects what you wear so seek advice on this. There are a number of unwritten social rules for dressing on dates. Don't be a victim of these, seek advice.

Unwritten appearance rules in the dating world

Appearance tips for females (by Gen)

- Always be yourself. Everyone has their own style, that is, what suits them in which they feel happy and confident.

- Many aspies have their own unique style and refuse to change it based on the rules of 'fashion'.

- However, on a first date it may be an idea to keep your style fairly neutral.

- 'Neutral' means clothes that are not 'too' anything – whether they be too tarty, too zany, too trendy, too conservative and so on.

- Try to choose an outfit that is attractive but doesn't stand out.

- When you get to know your date better then revert back to your usual style

- Freshly washed, nice smelling hair is a winner.

- A bit of natural make-up goes a long way even if you don't normally wear it.

- The 'natural' look seems to appeal to many, that is, make-up used to enhance your natural features rather than hide them or over-enhance them.

- If you need some help with finding appropriate looks or outfits look in fashion magazines and consult a trusted female friend who has a good eye for appearance.

Appearance tips for males (by Dean)

Don't:

- spend money on flash suits, or designer labels for the sake of impressing your date

- get the latest trendy look or haircut unless you really want to

- get body piercing, tattoos or other fashion fads just to impress
- wear clothes that are dirty, falling apart, too trendy or too bright, loud or faddy.

Do:

- make a basic effort with your appearance, this is enough
- wear the right fit of clothing
- always make an effort with tidiness for a date even if usually you are more 'laid-back' (the term laid back can apply to not shaving, leaving your hair uncut for a while, not regularly bathing, cutting nails, cleaning under fingernails, wearing the same outfit for a while without washing it)
- seek advice from a trusted friend who has a good knowledge of appearance.

Looking and behaving desperately

There is nothing unsexier than a desperate looking person. By 'desperate' here we refer to an individual who is so desperate to be in a relationship that they behave in an overly clingy and keen way toward any potential partners. Not looking desperate is socially sophisticated behaviour and quite an art. If you struggle with many social behaviours, as many Aspies do, social artistry and acting may not be for you. The best thing to do is to take the right attitude with you, which is 'If I meet someone nice, great, if I don't, oh well I am OK on my own for a while'. If you can be secure and independent enough being single, it is much more likely that you will attract an equal partner. Otherwise you may develop an unbalanced relationship, which involves over-depending on each other, behaving in a needy way and communicating that you can't cope without another half. These are all killers of healthy relationships. If you keep this 'happy in myself' attitude in mind, it will stave off constant ruminating over being single and a desperate attitude which will leave you single for much longer!

Chapter 3

Seeking and Finding Someone

In this chapter we discuss ways to meet
someone you like and issues around it.

Disclosing Asperger's syndrome

We would certainly advocate disclosing your AS to your partner. Your AS is a big part of who you are, which will affect how you live your life and make sense of the world. This of course does not have to be a negative thing. On the other hand, neither is AS your whole identity. You are an individual with AS, with an individual personality and self aside from your AS. We would advise always to be open about your AS in your relationship, but also never to dwell on it constantly.

The timing of disclosure, however is all-important. Many non-Aspies have never heard much of autism except perhaps in relation to children, let alone Asperger's syndrome. It would be best to disclose your AS when you have dated a few times and you have agreed to make the relationship official (this will be explained later). At this stage your partner would have seen enough of you to develop any feelings towards you and may be beginning to care about you, your happiness and welfare. Any earlier it could scare you partner off, any later, serious misunderstandings could occur. Having lived with AS you will know what the term 'serious misunderstanding' means. Educating (but not lecturing or going on endlessly about it) your partner about AS generally, and how it affects you individually is fundamental for the health of the budding relationship.

Choosing someone

It may, or may not seem obvious, but choosing someone you really like is essential. It is easy when seeking a partner to choose someone who is sexually attractive which is the thrill of lust, which is discussed later. However lust doesn't last forever, and what is left over at the end of this time is what determines whether your relationship will truly work. When choosing someone it is important to really get to know someone well before embarking on a serious relationship with them. There is nothing wrong with having a few 'flings' or short-term relationships to work out who the right person is for you from your experience. If you are embarking on a fling, always make sure that the other person is aware of the status of the relationship. Otherwise, you could be accused of being dishonest and cruel-hearted. Being deceitful always ends in tears.

They say 'opposites attract', but there still needs to be some common ground between you and your partner to work with. You don't have to have the same personality, but you do need to connect in some way, perhaps through a shared hobby or interest, or you may have similar values, beliefs or outlook on life. For example, one person may be highly religious and the other may not be but you still share a similar sense of morality.

Friendship and relationships

Some couples start out as friends first. Even for NTs it is not easy to start a relationship with someone the very day you first meet. The advantage of starting out as friends is that you get to know the other person platonically first and so feel more comfortable when you do eventually become partners. A relationship based on friendship is a good basis for a long-term relationship in that to be a friend of someone, you would usually 'like' them. However, being just a lover to someone does not have to be based on liking them as a person, it could simply be based upon sexual attraction and desire.

Relationships where both partners are friends as well as romantic partners seem to have high success rates. Many happy relationship testimonials seem to include one or both partners stating that their partner is their 'best friend'. It is very easy to confuse sexual attraction or lust with love. One of the main components of love that differs from lust is that you care deeply for that person's happiness and welfare, which is what a best friend would also do, added on top of that is sexual attraction, romance and passion which equate with friendship to a romantic and loving relationship.

As we discuss in Chapter 4, Dating, there are many ways to meet someone to date and maybe have a relationship with. Naturally having a relationship blossom out of friendship cuts out the whole 'finding someone' process. However, do not consider a possible relationship with someone you are not very keen on, as often when the subject of romance comes up in a relationship but one partner is not happy with that, it can ruin or end the original platonic friendship. Consider carefully how important a friendship is to you before deciding to take things further, if it goes wrong you could lose both. If you are in a group of friends and there happens to one member of the friendship group you would like to have a potential relationship with, it may be worth asking another friend what their opinion is before taking the plunge.

Approaching someone

This is something that anyone AS or not would find nerve wracking. If you worry about doing it too much it will become harder. It would be easier to approach someone who already knows you and might already be a friend. You could just ask them out for coffee or to the cinema, and give the impression it's just as friends. For example, "There's this film I want to see and I don't want to go on my own, would you like to see it?"

If you have no friends who you would consider a relationship with, then is there someone at work you could invite to have lunch with you during the lunch break one day? If you get on OK with the person, at worst you'll get a polite refusal, but they'll probably still thank you for asking them and feel pleased.

If friends and work are out, then the best suggestion is joining a group where you have a chance of meeting someone, or at least meeting someone who can introduce you to someone else who would go on dates with you.

You can always approach people you don't know, although if this is done in the street people are likely to be slightly bewildered or feel threatened. It would be best done in a social setting such as a bar or nightclub, but you should be aware of safety issues. Apparently, many people actually meet their partner in a supermarket, so if you try that tack and it works we'd love to hear about it.

If you are male there can be issues over being thought to be 'creepy' or 'sleazy'. You don't need to act like a 'ladies man' to approach someone. You should just begin with a simple, polite conversation. The best way is to make a comment about something relevant to the situation. If you meet them in a mutual interest situation you already have an advantage. If you meet at a pub or party you could comment on the music and then ask about the music they like. Then you could offer to buy them a drink and continue talking. If you see someone you like at a party it's nearly always OK to approach them and you could ask how they know the person throwing the party. From there conversation should run smoothly. Chat-up lines are an absolute no. Just don't bother. They are almost always taken negatively.

If you are female the same tips apply. We live in a world of male-female equality, so there should be no reason why a female should not approach a male. Some males may find this unique and love it; others may find it too forward. It really depends on the person you are approaching. Try to find out from someone who knows them what they are like first. If you can't do this, take the plunge, you have nothing to lose!

Where to meet someone

This is an age-old question, where opinion has a lot to contribute. It is dependent on age, culture, gender, sex, race and so on. In short, it is really very individual.

A night out

In the NT mainstream world 'going out on the pull' is a common thing to do. This involves going on a night out either to bars, pubs or nightclubs, drinking fair amounts of alcohol and engaging in a lot of flirting and many unwritten social rules. There is often a lot of sensory input (loud music, flickering lighting, crowds and so on) which can stress many Aspies out. Our opinion is this isn't an ideal one for Aspies. Many people on a night out are often after a bit of fun, i.e. a fling (short-term non-committed relationship, meeting for sex or simply a one-night stand).

At work

This again involves many unwritten social rules. Work relationships are often the focus of unpleasant gossip and scandal. Plus, being together and working together can be distracting and could be discouraged by bosses or supervisors. However, some relationships started through work can be successful especially if the partners work separately or in different departments.

Through friends

This is a good one if you have friends who have your best interests at heart and who know you well. Friends can often know people who they think may be suitable for you and through that can become a mutual friend. As outlined in the Friendship and Relationships section of this chapter, great long-lasting relationships are often based on solid friendships. If you struggle to get to know people, an introduction to a potential partner by a thoughtful friend can be a big help. Another good thing is that if a good friend or friends of yours know that you are on the lookout for a potential date you are building up the number of potential people that you will meet, rather than just looking on your own. Sometimes, if a good friend knows you well, they may have a more balanced, objective perspective of who would be suitable for you. It can be easy to be subjectively swayed by looks or hearsay about a potential date.

Through shared interests

We think this one is the best of all. As has already been discussed, many Aspies have strong and intense interests, which they will often talk about at significant length and which may take up a large part of their time. If you fall into this category, it may be worth considering meeting a partner through your special interest. If it takes up much of your time then a partner who is not into that interest could soon resent it and become bored with it. The positive aspect about meeting a partner through your interest is that you already have a safe bet that this won't happen and that you will already have plenty to talk about and do together. This can apply in real life or through Web groups.

Dating agencies

These can be expensive. Although they can lead to finding the right person, such agencies are notorious for being a waste of money. Meeting someone through chance or more spontaneous means appears to have a better success rate.

The online dating world

This is a potentially good means of meeting someone for Aspies and can work out cheaper than a dating agency. Some Internet dating services allow you to search their database for free but you may have to pay out to actually contact a member. This will usually be paid monthly by direct debit, so it could get pricey if you do not monitor the length of membership. Again, success rates don't seem to be as high as other means but could be a good starting point if you are socially inexperienced.

Speed dating

This seems to be quite popular at the moment. However some Aspies may find the speed of the process and the amount of people they may meet overloading and not compatible with AS traits. Plus, if you are a naturally quiet person this may be overwhelming as there is pressure to 'perform' in a short space of time, whereas you may take longer to show your true self. However, others may be happy with it.

Instant messaging services online

This is a good way to chat with lots of people platonically online, so you may find more people you relate to. But please observe Internet chatting safety rules for your own sake as you could be chatting to anyone. However, observing Internet safety advice should make for happy chatting. There are a few free providers of instant messaging; it is worth typing 'Instant Messaging Service' into any good search engine.

Chapter 4

Dating

**In this chapter we discuss what to do once
you've found and approached someone you
would like to date.**

The first date

Once you have found a 'date' (someone to go out with!) the next task is to pick where to go. As many Aspies like to know what is going to happen ahead of them and dislike uncertainty and surprises, it may be a good idea to discuss beforehand with your date over the phone what you will be doing. If you are uncomfortable on the phone, texting or emailing may be better. By agreeing on what you will be doing you have already 'broken the ice', that is, made initial contact, which will make you feel more relaxed with each other when you do eventually go on your date together.

The cinema or theatre

This is a good one for Aspies, especially if you suffer from social anxiety or shyness. It also avoids problems with eye contact and reading non-verbal language. When the film or performance is over it is good for a talking point. Be careful though over the type of film or performance you choose to see as this could make either one of you uncomfortable if it is controversial. Choosing a film or performance together gives an easy early conversation point and gets you both interacting in a simple social way.

A meal

This could cause problems especially if you are anxious about eating in public as some Aspies can be. Eating in a formal restaurant does involve a number of unwritten social rules and etiquette. Eating in less formal places such as in a pleasant pub or café-bar can be less daunting. Many Aspies are quite picky about foods, certain combinations of foods or may need to have a special diet, such as a gluten and casein-free diet. These needs can all add up to some difficulty when choosing something on a menu. The anxiety, which may be caused by indecision or eating unsuitable food on a date, can be negative. Choose carefully where you go out to eat on a date and it may be an idea to check beforehand that there will be something suitable for you to eat.

A few drinks

This is fine provided an appropriate venue is chosen. A few drinks can certainly help conversation flow, but overdoing it could be disastrous as you may lose control over your social behaviour, especially if you normally struggle with it. You may need to stay sober if you are trying extra-hard with socially appropriate behaviours.

Double dating

This is a good idea if you have an understanding friend. If they are aware of your potential problems, they can be on hand to give advice such as on appropriate social behaviour and help the interaction run smoothly by leading joint conversations, filling in awkward silences and ensuring that any non-verbal language signals are not missed. Regular short discussions with the friend on the progress of the date and advice-giving could be done, say when getting drinks at the bar to make sure that the date is unaware of it. Good places for double dates are bowling alleys, or going to see live music.

Conversation on the date

Something many Aspies appear to struggle with is making 'small talk', or general conversation. Aspies are great at talking with a specific purpose such as lecturing, or talking about a special interest. Don't worry too much if you struggle with making appropriate conversation or with keeping it going. A good point to remember is that most people love to talk about themselves much more than they like to listen to others. Use this to your advantage. Many people are very flattered when someone asks them questions about themselves and listen more in a conversation than talk. The best approach to conversation on a date is to ask as many genuine questions about your date as you can think of. Be genuinely interested in what they have to say about themselves and they will love it.

While they talk, the pressure is off you to make the majority of the conversation. It is a good idea to practise thinking of good questions you could ask before the date with a friend. As long as the questions are not too personal, but rather more general, you should definitely win them over. After all, one thing many partners in a relationship moan about is never being listened to!

Good questions to ask are:

● What do you think of it here?
  (wherever you happen to be on your date)

● So, do you work?
  (If they say yes, say, 'I'd love to hear more about what you do.')

● What do you like to do when you aren't at work,
  what are your interests?

Be aware that controversial topics such as religion, morals, politics, money, sex or past relationships might make conversation difficult.

Don't spend the entire time being boastful. Just be natural. Even if you think you are a big bore in a conversation, your partner might be fascinated by what you have to say. However, don't take the entire conversation over. Make sure that your date gets the chance to speak; otherwise they could think that you're self absorbed or simply not interested in them. At the same time, don't leave your date to do all the talking because they might think you have something to hide, nothing to say or that you are not interested in them. They'll have no incentive to meet you again, if they know no more about you after the date than they did before. If you do struggle to talk about yourself and your date questions why you are quiet, just say, 'Well I'd rather hear about you than me', to give you a get-out.

Always keep conversation upbeat, positive and light-hearted on a date. Leave deep, controversial or negative issues for when you know each other better. If you are unsure of any of the points made in this section, check them out and practise them with someone socially able and whom you trust.

Flirting

Aspies, as you will be aware, struggle with non-verbal language which includes eye contact, body language, tone of voice, speed of voice intonation, and gestures. Flirting is an art based on all of these non-verbal behaviours. Therefore reading others' flirting and flirting yourself may prove difficult and confusing.

Consider the following figures:

- 55% of the impression we get from someone comes through body language

- 38% is from the tone, speed and intonation (pitch) of our voice

- 7% is from what we actually say!

No wonder communication is tough for Aspies who struggle with the 93% of non-verbal communication! We are not suggesting that you should not engage in flirting and attempting to read the non-verbal language of love and attraction! You may need to do some intensive reading and learning about body language and flirting first of all. There are many good body language books on the market so why not read some of them to improve.

Also it may be worth talking with trusted NT friends who are aware of your non-verbal language difficulties. Ask them for some tips. If you know that you could be potentially socially inappropriate forget the idea of flirting until you are more sure of yourself.

It's fine to try a bit of flirting on the date. It would be pointless going on a date if you expect your date not to flirt. It could be tricky for an Aspie to know how to flirt, but a good way to start would be by making various compliments. Your date might not mind if you're a bit 'cheeky' as long as you don't do or say anything inappropriate. There is a big difference between being cheeky and socially inappropriate which could ruin things. Some flirting could involve touch, but be sure first that your date is OK with this.

Safety

When you're meeting someone new on a date, ALWAYS put safety first. You shouldn't go off anywhere with your date other than public places and you shouldn't get into a car with them or reveal your address unless they know it anyway. It's always better to meet in public places initially rather than at someone's house that you don't know. It's a good idea to tell someone where you're expecting to go and if you can to take a mobile phone. If you do happen to feel unsafe at any part of the date, you should get out of there straight away.

Aspies do struggle with many aspects of communication, and as a result it makes it very hard to read social situations and the intentions of others. Don't let this leave you vulnerable. Aspies find it much harder than NTs who tend to rely on their natural innate instincts, which those with AS tend to lack. Talk things through with a trusted socially able friend or supporter. Ask them to give you tips on reading people and situations, and ask them perhaps to be around the vicinity of the location of the date – not to check up on you but so that they can be around nearby to support you should you feel unsure or vulnerable.

However, don't go on a date with a fearful or overly anxious attitude. If you get to know as much as possible about the person before you go, there shouldn't be any problems as long as you follow basic date-safety advice as above. Being overly anxious can make relaxing very hard and can make both you and your date feel uncomfortable.

The second date

This would usually be a bit less formal than the first date. You should be able to relax a bit more and there will probably be some physical contact on the date if things are going well and your date may allow you to be intimate. Don't analyze it too much though, and don't have a set plan on how to interact, just go along and go with the flow. Dinner would be ideal for a second date, but of course it's entirely up to you and your date.

The third date onwards

If you've got this far, you must be doing something right. Further physical contact will almost certainly be acceptable, but first make sure your date is comfortable with this. At this point you may decide together whether you want to actually have a relationship with that person. If you are going to choose to enter into a relationship together make sure that you want the same things out of it to avoid misunderstandings or upset. You may still wish to date a bit more to decide.

Making it official

If you've met a few times and are getting on well, it's a good sign though you should have an open mind. It would be all too easy to read signs which are not there, but by the same token many Aspies struggle to read any signs plus may have such low confidence that they could easily be oblivious to someone liking them. These days, it's considered OK for the female to do the asking but many still leave that up to the male. Don't be put off asking someone out for fear of rejection. If you've come this far, they will probably be more than happy to go out with you officially, and if they do say no, it will almost certainly be polite and if not, that's their problem and you wouldn't want a partner without manners. Never take rejection too personally; there could be many reasons for this, which may not even be related to you. It is better to take the attitude 'oh well, that's their loss, they don't know what they're missing out on.' If they do seem to be happy with you, it would be enough to say, 'Shall we make the relationship official?' This should clarify for both of you that you are a couple so that both of you are clear on the status of your relationship. You could make the day romantic if that is what you are both into. It could be a very memorable day!

Tips for after having made the relationship official:

- Ring your partner but not too often – everyone has different opinions on telephone contact so ask them what they are comfortable with.

- If the phone is difficult for you to use, tell them to avoid misunderstandings. Ask if you could email or text instead.

- Share interests if appropriate.

- Don't overspend on lavish presents. Small thoughtful gifts now and then are usually well received though.

- Show genuine interest and concern in each other's lives.

- Make them feel special. If you are unsure how to do this, ask your partner, 'You are really special to me, how can I show you?'

- Tell your partner how you feel. Even Aspies can do this. It's easier to say 'I love you' or 'I have feelings for you' to a partner than anyone else. It's not soppy, it's normal and natural.

- If you can't articulate your feelings face to face, write them down and show them to your partner. It is fine to use email or texting for this.

- You don't need to say how you feel every day to your partner but say it often enough so that they know how you feel. Even if once seems enough to you, hearing it often to others is preferable.

- If you find telling a partner 'I love you' desperately hard, saying it in another language takes off the pressure and keeps things fun and light-hearted.

General dating etiquette

- Don't 'play it too cool', i.e. look like you're not interested at all.

- Don't 'play too hard to get' – just be yourself if you overdo it your apparent lack of interest will be taken literally.

- Always ask relevant questions, see Conversation on the date.

- If possible find out from their friends what they think of you.

- However, don't talk about or brag about your date to your friends because if they find out they may be offended.

- Always be pleasant and responsible. This is attractive.

- Use humour but not immature or crude humour to be on the safe side.

- If your sense of humour is underdeveloped gain tips from trusted friends.

- If you smoke – don't smoke while eating together unless you have asked first.

- Don't smoke generally without asking permission first from your date.

- Don't drink or smoke to excess until you know your date well enough.

- Avoid ordering meals that are complicated or messy to eat.

- Try using good table manners even if you are not used to them.

- Don't talk during the film.

- Don't make physical contact until you are sure it's OK with your date.

- For initial physical contact test out relations between you by touching their arm or hand, or say, 'Is it ok if I put my arm around you?'

- To initiate kissing it is probably safest to initially peck your date on the cheek, if you are not rebuffed try pecking them on the lips. If they seem OK with this try a more prolonged, intimate kiss.

- If this seems too stressful just simply ask, 'Is it OK if I kiss you?'

Sex

This is a complicated one. It is one of the most natural instincts of the human race, but it also one of the most often talked about and debated subjects in society. Sex really is very individual. It is strongly related to complex beliefs such as religion, cultural differences, racial differences, sexual preferences, upbringing, past experiences, gender differences and so on. The advice given here is general and consistent with the authors' personal views. Your views may be different, that is the whole essence of the individual nature of sexual beliefs.

Ideally, sex should be associated with love. Naturally, it is also associated with lust. The differences between love and lust will be discussed in Chapter 5, Maintaining. The social rules surrounding sex are notoriously complicated, often contradictory and subject to humour but also to deep debate. NB We are not going to give a complete listing of social rules and sex. This is because this would be too definitive and we are wishing to keep this general and not subjective. However, the following general rules are a good starting point. Beyond these, it is best to seek advice from trusted friends in your own circumstances.

- Many females, and some males, associate sex more with emotion than as a purely physical act. Make sure that you and your partner are sufficiently close emotionally as well as physically so that you don't get hurt.

- Always, always ensure that safe sex is observed with correctly used contraception.

- Ideally, sex should be a reflection of love, however some people are happy with sex that is purely based on lust. Make sure if this is the case that your partner is aware of the situation.

- Ideally, sex should occur in a long-term committed relationship; however this is not always the case. If you choose to have sex outside of a long-term relationship, always take responsibility for emotional or physical consequences when the relationship breaks up.

- Always consider that sex could lead to pregnancy as contraception can fail in a heterosexual relationship. Be prepared to discuss what you would do if this ever occurred.

- Never, ever have sex unless you are ready. No means no. Never be pressured.

- Don't have sex just because your partner may want to, the choice to have a sexual relationship must be a joint decision.

You don't have to engage in sex to be intimate. Here are some great ways to be intimate which don't involve sex:

- Non-sexual touch, for example, a massage

- kissing, not always in obvious places – consider the whole person, for example, the hair or the face may get neglected

- holding each other by candlelight

- enjoying food you have made together.

Chapter 5

Maintaining

In this chapter we discuss what happens when you have got together with that person you like and how to maintain a successful relationship.

Having fun together

You are with each other because you enjoy each other's company and can make each other happy. The best way to get enjoyment out of each other's company is to have fun together whether you create your own entertainment without leaving the house, or go out for the day or night or choose a fun leisure activity such as swimming or dancing. Doing something like this once in a while, helps to make the relationship a happy one. Some of the time having fun together involves intimacy and quality time alone, or it could involve others too. Agreeing together on what is fun for both of you is most important. It defeats the object if you disagree on what 'fun' is!

Here are some ideas for fun times together:

- a spontaneous short break somewhere together, there are plenty of bargain breaks on the Internet

- a physical activity such as ice-skating, horse-riding or bowling

- spending the day at a health farm

- a luxury night out at a ball, or the opera

- baking a cake together

- outdoor extreme sports such as snowboarding, abseiling or white-water rafting

- a day at a theme park

- a romantic night in with candlelight, rose petals spread around, a massage and feeding each other luxury foods

- a simple walk in the country

- a pillow fight!

These are just suggestions, getting together to think of something fun to do can be fun and creative in itself!

Caring about someone

You need to give thought to how the other person is feeling, and be ready to comfort them if they are upset. You should be careful not to do or say anything which they may find hurtful. If you think a certain action could potentially hurt your partner's feelings, then don't do it. You shouldn't put them in a situation that they may find uncomfortable, and you need to be prepared to protect them from dangers.

Some Aspies, either before or after diagnosis, may not have been used to having someone around to care for. As many Aspies well know, through either having being bullied, excluded or isolated, time alone is often not a choice but imposed on them. If you have not had much practice in caring about someone through any of these situations, don't worry. Everyone has the capacity to care for someone whether they have had the opportunity before or not. Many Aspies are really friendly and caring but rarely get the chance to show it as they are often shunned for being 'odd', 'weird' and so on. If you have felt shunned and excluded in your life, just remember that it is the people who are excluding you who will lose out. Be strong in the fact that you are not so arrogant and cruel-hearted. When the right person comes along who accepts you as you are, caring about them will come naturally.

Change

Change is something that those on the autistic spectrum are seen to have trouble with. Change is natural in relationships. Change in relationships reflects the changes that inevitably occur in every individuals' life. You will both change in different ways. Often for the better. If not for the better, then both of you will need to learn to live with the changes in each other. It is best not to fight against change, as it is a natural process. Sometimes, unfortunately when one partner changes in ways the other can't deal with, then breaking up may be the only option.

You may find that you and your partner are not as compatible as you originally thought. If your partner ended the relationship, this was not necessarily anything to do with your Asperger's syndrome, but even if it was, that doesn't have to mean that everyone else would share the same view as your ex-partner. It could be that the factor that ended your previous relationship, could be the same factor that will attract the next person to you, as each individual reacts to things in different ways. Rather then try to change something about yourself that you can't help, try to find someone who will accept you as you are. If you have AS, this can be harder to find, but persevering is essential. You will get there in the end. The more positive you are, the more likely it will be that this will happen.

Quality time

Quality time refers to putting time aside especially for you and your partner to give solely to the relationship between you both. You need to spend some time alone with your partner as often as possible. This gives the best possible chance to appreciate what you have and enjoy each other's company. This is what relationships are about and makes them very special. You should never get too complacent in a relationship, because your partner might feel that you're not giving them enough attention. It seems that the more time is given to a relationship, the better it is. This does not mean that if you both lead busy lives that your relationship will be doomed to failure. Having quality time little and often is better than none at all, even if it is only 15 minutes snatched when you can. The act of spending quality time together is the most important factor as it shows that no matter how little time you have together, the health of the relationship is high on your list of priorities.

Ideas for quality time together:

- a brisk walk in the park holding hands
- watching a video by candlelight together
- taking an afternoon off work or study to be alone together
- playing a computer game together
- anything you enjoy doing as long as it is together!

Romance and affection

A classic Aspie stereotype points to an individual who dislikes sentimentality, has no concept of romance and does not see the point of affection. Certainly from our own experience we as individuals don't fit into this stereotypical persona. Romance, affection and sentimentality are not absolutes that have to be a part of a relationship to make it work. It depends mostly on the needs of each individual. If neither of you like romance, affection or sentimentality then opt out of it by all means. If one of you likes it but the other doesn't, try at least to compromise for both of your needs to be met.

To be affectionate and romantic you don't have to indulge in great sentimental acts, small gestures are equally as important, such as:

- putting small romantic messages on post-it notes around the house, or in each other's pockets

- making a meal together or as a surprise for your partner

- buying your partner something you know they want but didn't expect.

Intimacy and touch

Firstly, you will need to have an idea of how your partner feels about these issues and it's important that they respect your limitations. For example, let them know if you need to be warned in advance if you are going to touch them, otherwise they will think you are being cold with them and think they've done something to upset you. If even a hug from a partner makes you go stiff, you'll need to make them aware that it's not them you have an issue with, but hugging in general. It is quite common for some individuals on the autistic spectrum to be sensitive to touch. They could prefer hard or soft touch, or perhaps infrequent or very frequent touch. It is best to check this out with your partner first.

If you are very uncomfortable with certain forms of intimacy and touch from your partner then you would be best advised to tell them that you can cope with intimacy and touch if it is on your terms. If your partner is another Aspie and has their own set of limitations, they'll probably understand your limits as they could be similar.

Intimacy, however, doesn't just apply to touch. Intimacy can be created by doing thoughtful things for each other such as romantic or well-thought-out gestures such as putting your feelings down in writing. Many Aspies find it easier to communicate thoughts and feelings in writing so this could be a useful way of being intimate if you feel uncomfortable face-to-face. Even a quick text or email saying how you feel is enough. Another option if you are happy talking face-to-face is to sit down together and just catch up on each other's news and latest views; this can create intimacy if normally you are both quite busy or don't talk that much.

Disagreements

Unless you are two of the most mild mannered people in the world, you'll never be able to agree on everything. Disagreements are a part of life and no one can avoid them without running away from their problems.

Nearly all couples have disagreements and it's often a healthy part of a relationship. You should always try to see the argument from your partner's point of view. For Aspies seeing things from another person's point of view, or having empathy is something that doesn't come easily if you are not used to it. Aspies are seen to be naturally lacking in 'Theory of Mind', or being naturally empathic. This may be something initially you may have to force yourself to do. It is certainly possible to teach yourself to empathize with others. If you have great difficulty with seeing things only from your own point of view you may need to seek a good psychotherapist who understands the autistic spectrum who may be able to support you in learning how to empathize with others. To avoid constant arguments in a relationship, it is essential that you learn how to empathize. Empathy doesn't have to totally be innate to be effective.

The important thing is how you handle the disagreements. Even if you don't agree with your partner's opinion, you should at least try to understand where they are coming from, and you should try to reach a compromise. A healthy relationship is unlikely to fail on the basis of a single disagreement or argument unless there is violence involved. Never, ever become physically violent with a partner. You may feel so angry or frustrated that you might feel like being violent, but actually carrying this out is a serious offence. Violence in relationships or 'domestic violence' is now being taken more seriously by the police. There is never, ever an excuse for verbal, emotional or physical abuse in ANY circumstances. If you find it very hard to control your anger with a partner, please do seek help.

Communication

As AS is a condition that mainly affects communication, key issues for a relationship to resolve will concern communication. Open, honest, straightforward communication is absolutely essential for a successful relationship. Many Aspies are lucky that they seem to be naturally straightforward, open and honest, sometimes too honest! However, the bit there seems to be a problem with is communicating these sentiments. The best thing to do to overcome communication problems is to be aware of how they affect you based on the following list. Then to seek support from an AS trained counsellor or psychotherapist with your communication difficulties.

1. Slow processing speed of communication.

2. Trouble with understanding social nuances and unwritten rules of communication.

3. Literal language interpretation.

4. Literal interpretation of social communication.

5. Problems using the telephone – written communication, texting, or email may be used if face-to-face contact is difficult.

6. Non-verbal communication comprehension difficulties.

In any relationship, you need to communicate with each other regularly. Talking is essential, even if it is just general conversation, but you should both check that things are OK with the relationship from your partner's point of view. If you are concerned that your partner is holding something back, a good question to ask them is, 'Are we OK?' If there is any aspect of the relationship that is bothering you, you need to mention this to your partner rather than to let it fester and possibly grow so big that it can't be resolved. If you're worried that your partner will react badly to something you could well be surprised and therefore relieved. If they don't take your news well you should at least be proud of your honesty, and unless it's something really bad your partner will probably forgive you if you knew you were at fault. It is far better to tell them what is bothering you because if they are fine with what you've told them you'll be relieved and feel happier. Even if they don't react well to what you tell them through your honesty, at least if you have a strong relationship it will probably survive the problem.

Partnership

There are two people in any relationship and you both need to work together at it. You share every aspect of each other's lives and help and support each other through good times and bad. Quite often your partner is your soulmate and you tell each other everything and share your problems with each other good and bad. Another way to look at partnership is that you are a team; you work together for a mutual goal using both of your individual strengths. Aspies are known to prefer to operate alone rather than as part of a team. This may be true in terms of work or leisure. However when love is involved the need to be independent all of the time tends to lessen. This is because when in love you want to be with the person a lot of the time. Even as an Aspie you can still feel this, even if not to the same intense amount as an NT might.

Being a partnership also means striving for mutual dreams and goals as well as working together to work through everyday life. Being a successful partnership can be very rewarding in that you can achieve more together and enjoy helping and supporting each other. Partnership will strengthen your relationship. There is a difference between being a partnership and just being two individuals who happen to be in a relationship together.

Love

This is a really tricky one! The definition of love has been debated for as long as time began. We're certainly not going to give it! Love is often confused with lust, which is purely sexual attraction and desire and is short-term. Love is much rarer than lust and is something that grows and many would say needs work for it to last. Differences between love and lust are certainly a matter of opinion; love is individual to each couple. Love and lust can also occur together at some points in a relationship. In the long-term however love is all-important.

The two should not be confused but often are. Lust refers to loving the ideal fantasy idea of a person whereas love is genuinely caring for the person just as they are and wanting to share everything with them and care deeply about them. Love is a very powerful emotion, whereas lust is being sexually attracted to the person and longing for intimacy and touch with them but not actually feeling emotionally attached to the person.

The following list identifies some things you may experience with love and lust.

Lust:

- thinking of your partner first and foremost in terms of their sexual attractiveness

- yearning for physical intimacy with them over anything else

- wanting excitement and passion with them over real life boring, everyday things or difficult times

- you imagine them as you would like them to be rather than as they are.

Love:

- liking your partner as a whole person as well as for their sexual attractiveness

- wanting to be with your partner all of the time whatever you are doing together

- caring deeply for their welfare and happiness

- thinking of loving your partner just as they are in reality 'warts and all'

- wanting to be together through good and bad times

- being willing to do anything to keep them and to make them happy

- you would support them whatever happened

- you feel attached to them and could never imagine being apart from them

- you feel empathy towards them.

Chapter 6

The Long-term

In this chapter we discuss what happens when you have been together in a relationship for a while and where you go from there.

Are we going the same way?

You both need to be looking for the same things out of the relationship. If you want a casual relationship and your partner wants a serious one, it is not going to work. You will have an idea of what you want in your relationship. For example, one person might want children and the other might not. Going the same way does not mean that you should have exactly the same dreams, beliefs, hopes, morals and so on. As long as you can compromise enough to fulfil each other's needs this should be sufficient. However, some people cannot compromise with their plans and this may cause a split. Many Aspies are very involved in their work or interests and this needs to be considered if you are both to want a career and a family. Both of you can't do absolutely everything you hope to do in life as well as dealing with the responsibility of being together.

At this stage of the relationship you may decide to look to the long-term together or split to go in separate ways. Splitting up does not mean that you no longer love each other. A long-term relationship involves not only love but fulfilling your dreams and hopes for your lives together. If you can't agree on fulfilling both of your hopes and dreams with a compromise, then it may be better to split than carry on hoping that you will. Always be honest when discussing whether you are both going the same way. Deceiving your partner will come out even if you think it won't. Staying together in the short-term as it seems harder to split, even though your long-term plans are separate, will set you up for heartache the longer you stay together. Splitting up can be emotionally draining in that you may have been together for a long time and adjusting to such a big change could be very hard. Don't be tempted to get back together if the initial change is hard. Many people on the autistic spectrum find change notoriously hard to deal with. However, if you made a decision to split rather than stay together in the long-term, working through the difficult short-term apart will be easier than making the mistake of staying together long-term when you both know deep down that it is wrong for you.

If you have decided that you can fulfil your hopes and dreams in your relationship together in the long-term then you have done very well and your love must be very strong. The best of luck to you!

Co-habiting

If you're in a serious relationship you might consider moving in together. This is something that has to be considered very carefully because you will be spending most of your free time together, will share responsibility for looking after the house and will probably share finances and perhaps have a joint bank account. You will need to be prepared to put up with each other's bad habits and strange quirks that you normally may not see. Remember, this would be a huge commitment and best not rushed into.

Co-habiting is seen as a step along the way to deciding whether you really want to make a life-long commitment to one another. Co-habiting is a good way of getting to know your partner through and through, 'warts and all', which refers to every side of your partner, good and bad. Many people decide after living together for a while that it is time for them to make a long-term commitment either through marriage or otherwise. Others decide that they aren't right together in the long-term. It is perfectly acceptable nowadays to live together outside of marriage or long-term commitment. It is often better to do things this way round rather than making a long-term commitment and then realizing you are wrong for each other. There is more to a long-term commitment than love and having fun together. You are involved in every aspect of each other's life: the good and bad times and the boring, serious stuff as well, such as finances and sharing bills and so on.

Marriage

We can't really advise on marriage as neither of us are, or have been, married! However, there are a couple of good books on the market discussing the issues involving in an Aspergian marriage. We recommend having a look at these if you are considering marriage. Naturally, due to AS being a difference in social interaction, communication and imagination, the issue of marriage is one to think about seriously. However, that does not mean that it isn't going to work! Having AS, as we have explored in this guide, does not have to be a barrier to happy and successful relationships, and it should not preclude marriage.

Some people may wish to seek genetic counselling due to the unconfirmed possibility of Asperger or autistic children being born should you be considering children in marriage. However, as we know, AS itself is essentially a 'difference'; it becomes a 'disability' when it is seen only negatively, or associated with co-occurring learning disabilities or other psychological or physical disorders.

Marriage should only be considered if you're very serious about spending the rest of your life with your partner. People ideally only marry when they are in love with each other. You don't have to save up forever to get married but it would help to be comfortably off first.

Some people don't believe in marriage as they feel they don't need 'a bit of paper' to prove their love and commitment to each other. This is fine if your partner shares the same view but many people, religious or not, may wish to marry at some point in their life. Then of course you need to be certain that you want the same things out of your married life together. On a more trivial but important note, the issue of what type of wedding has to be considered; your partner might have always dreamed of a white wedding and you might dread the idea but you should be able to compromise!

Chapter 7

Case-studies

In this chapter we look at two real life stories of relationships from one female and one male AS adult.

Case-study 1

Name: Andrew

Age: 21

Gender: Male

When diagnosed with AS: March 2001 (age 17)

Questions

1. Are you currently in a relationship?

No.

2. Have you had previous relationships?

No. I have met up with a few girls from my local area over the last couple of years, whom I had got to know through the Internet. I did enjoy their company; however, none of them was interested in a relationship. I now only keep in touch with one of them. I haven't had any luck in dating anyone that I have met through friends at school or university.

3. How does AS affect your relationships?

n/a

4. What are the negative ways AS affects your relationships?

n/a

5. What are the positive ways AS impacts on your relationships?

n/a

6. What help would you require to support a successful relationship?

As someone who is only mildly affected by Asperger's syndrome, I imagine that I will not require a great deal of support when (or if) I get into a relationship with a woman. A lot of my difficulties stem from feeling lonely and wanting a relationship but not feeling confident enough about myself, and knowing how to recognize an opportunity when it arises. I am far more out-going when with just one other person (male, as well as female), than

I am in groups. I think that if I did meet a woman who was willing to be in a relationship with me, and accepted me for who I am, then I should not encounter any more problems than the average man of my age.

7. Do you think gender affects how AS individuals succeed in relationships?

This is only my perception, but I think that AS females have an advantage over AS males when it comes to finding a partner. I believe this is due to the way society generally functions and having spoken with a number of AS females over the Internet and in real life, they are happy to accept my point of view. Whilst there are of course exceptions to this, I have realized in life that men seem to be far more likely to approach a potential partner than women are to do the opposite. When I've been out to nightclubs with friends from university, it always seems to me that there are plenty of men wandering around looking to dance with a woman, whereas women don't seem to approach men. I often find that women, who are perhaps single, tend to dance with other women and from my experience, aren't interested in dancing with me! This may be due to my body language.

8. Do you like affection, romance or sentimentality?

To be honest, until I've had the experience of a relationship, I cannot really give a definite answer to this question. I certainly feel that I would be a sensitive, romantic kind of partner for somebody. I suppose I could draw some comparisons with my love for my pets, or other people's animals. Of course, the relationship one has with one's pets is different from a relationship with another person, but in terms of the companionship animals can provide, I imagine I would feel the same emotions if I had a partner to keep me company.

9. How do you feel about physical contact in a relationship?

Everyone who has AS is different from one another in the way they are affected, even though there are commonly recognized traits. As far as I am concerned, I do not notice any obvious sensory issues. I am perfectly comfortable with physical contact, in a relationship, or not. From the little experience I have had of spending time alone with women, I have enjoyed cuddles and kisses and holding hands (none of these occasions led to a relationship but I'm glad I was able to achieve something even if they never lasted).

10. Do you feel comfortable with emotional interaction?

I think this issue is a tricky one to discuss, having not yet been in a relationship and having only limited experience of it in terms of emotional interaction with potential girlfriends. With family and friends however, I am relatively comfortable, though I have learnt that I can sometimes come across as fairly emotionless and appear to be unaware of other people's feelings, wants and needs. As I write this, I am feeling much more positive about life than I was a few weeks ago and I have noticed that my inner feelings affect the way I interact with others, in that I am much more socially outgoing when I'm not depressed.

11. Do you hope to marry or have a long-term relationship?

For several years I have been longing for a relationship. I have been told on numerous occasions that I'm only young and my time will come, though it has been very frustrating seeing others, perhaps more than five years younger than me, in relationships. Granted, many people of 15 or 16 are unlikely to stay in one relationship, leading to marriage and will probably suffer a few upsets from unfaithful partners, but it's all about experience. I feel like my teenage years have completely passed me by and I've missed out on a lot of good times. I don't expect to suddenly jump into a long-term relationship, ending in marriage with the first person that I go out with, though I suppose this could well happen, particularly as I get older and women are looking to settle down. I would love to get married eventually, as I think that having a wife would be great company and support for me – something which I could never achieve through friends alone.

12. Would you like to have a family?

I would love to have children one day. Hopefully before I'm 40, as I don't want to be too old before they have reached adulthood!

13. Do you feel that a relationship with someone else with AS or a similar personality would be preferable?

I have thought a lot about this issue over the past year or two and I tend to change my mind quite often. I suppose with no experience of either situation, then I cannot say for sure and of course, everyone is different, AS or not. My general thoughts are that I feel a relationship with an understanding person, without AS, would be preferable. When I'm functioning well, I am able to socialize comfortably with neurotypical friends and acquaintances and I imagine that having a partner who is slightly more outgoing than me could be beneficial for me.

14. Do you feel pressure to be in a relationship by society?

Until I became a university student, I attended an all-boys school between the ages of 12 and 18. Before 12, I wasn't really mature enough to understand the concept of love and relationships, however, since coming to university this issue has led me into a lot of depression. Until very recently, I used to bottle all these feelings up and make excuses for my depression, blaming it on the pressures of the course I study, whereas to a much greater extent, it was because I had become desperately obsessed by wanting to find a partner. I have wasted hundreds of hours searching through Internet dating sites and similar, hoping that someone living near me would find me interesting and want to meet up. As explained earlier, I did succeed a number of times in meeting girls around my age in the local area; however I believe my naivete and general appearance let me down. In all cases, I was told, "You're a nice guy but can we just be friends?" This did lead to a lot of upset and depression for me, after the short-lived happiness. Lately, I had begun to ask myself whether women are worth bothering with as they seem to complicate everything in my eyes. Why can't they just chill out and have some fun? I'm not asking every girl I meet to marry me!

15. Do you feel you have sufficient empathy to have a relationship?

As for this final question, I think I'll have to wait and see! I don't think I lack completely in empathy, however I do admit to being perhaps slightly more self-centred than I should be, though I believe this has been brought on by depression and negative feelings, which I am working hard to move away from.

I hope my account has been useful for many of you reading this. I think it's important to bear in mind that although you may be a fellow Aspie you may see things completely differently from me. I have learnt since being diagnosed that we're all as different from one another as neurotypical people. Nevertheless, I would like to think that my story can be a useful guide.

Case-study 2

Name; Mand Harrison

Age: 25

Gender: Female

When diagnosed with AS: September 2003 (aged 24)

Questions

1. Are you currently in a relationship?

Yes, I have been in my current relationship for three-and-a-half years and we married eight months ago.

2. Have you had previous relationships?

I have been in a continuous string of relationships from the age of 14 onwards. I recall that my female friends seemed to get quite annoyed that they hardly ever saw me outside of school because of the way I would 'disappear' into each of my relationships. With hindsight I understand that I must have felt more secure in a one-to-one situation, which is why my preference was always to be with a partner as opposed to socializing in wider peer groups.

3. How does AS affect your relationships?

I have always been insecure which means I need a great deal of reassurance from my partners in order that I feel able to trust them. At the same time I also need a lot of time on my own so that I can get things done in my own way without any distractions. In the past I imagine these behaviours must have made me seem like I was 'blowing hot and cold' or that relationships with me were one-sided. Since getting my diagnosis, having a relationship has been a lot easier as I am able to understand myself so much more and my husband and I can accept me for who I am instead of my keeping on trying and failing to be something else.

4. What are the negative ways AS affects your relationships?

AS has been detrimental to all my past relationships in the same way, because I am unable to 'feel' my partner's emotions, I rely entirely on what he says to me in words and somehow words alone are never enough. This makes me harass him for love and attention when I need it, and yet when he offers it of his own accord (when I am not expecting it) it can make me feel trapped so I just want to escape.

In the past, this would lead to my partner playing emotional mind games to 'get back at me' in the same way it seemed I was playing him. This would generally escalate pretty quickly resulting in a volatile relationship consisting of turbulent highs and lows – never a dull moment! In the end I would reach the end of my emotional tether and cut my losses, severing the relationship in order to recover and maintain my sanity.

Knowing that I have AS has given me the freedom of acceptance, I no longer feel the need to fight the tide with such ferocity as I used to. Don't get me wrong, I still and probably always will have a stormy relationship, but the negativity doesn't get out of hand anywhere near as much as it once did and when it does, we both know not to take it personally.

5. What are the positive ways AS impacts on your relationships?

My husband respects my genuine, open, honest nature. Over the years he has seen for himself that I don't lie or cheat and that I always say things exactly the way they are. He knows that he can trust me implicitly and makes a point of telling me, which, over time has helped me to reciprocate trust in him.

I have my own peculiar sense of humour (and my own use of language according to my husband) that he has really grown to appreciate and be delighted by. My ways have started to 'rub off on him' and he says he could never have an NT relationship again. Seen from the NT point of view a relationship with an Aspie can be a lot of hard work but the rewards make it all worthwhile in the end.

6. What help would you require to support a successful relationship?

Understanding is the key. An information source for Aspies and their partners would be a great help, provided that it steers away from the negative connotations associated with words such as 'disorder', 'suffering' and 'impairment'. I believe that AS needs to be portrayed in a more balanced way, highlighting the positive aspects as well as the negative.

I think it would be useful for partners of Aspies to have an online community where they can find reassurance from other people in their situation. This kind of support, from 'real' people can offer invaluable information and ideas that aren't in any text book, it would also highlight the vast differences between one Aspie and the next – something that a partner may not even consider if he/she has only experience of a single Aspie individual.

7. Do you think gender affects how AS individuals succeed in relationships?

I think that generally female Aspies have a greater chance of forming relationships with the opposite sex for several different reasons, mostly based around social preconceptions we all have about gender and appropriate behaviour. Firstly, I believe that society is more accepting of shyness in women than in men and that this vulnerability displayed in a woman appeals to the protective side of a man's nature. I think even in today's society, it is not considered masculine to be quiet and shy, and sadly this may discourage some women from ever even thinking about becoming involved with an Aspie man.

On the flip-side to being shy, Aspies can also be very outspoken on occasion and generally get straight to the point when talking about things. Again I believe this is a trait that is more likely to be appreciated by the male mind, whereas women may consider such bluntness to be sheer insensitivity.

8. Do you like affection, romance or sentimentality?

Yes, it means a lot to me that someone cares about me enough to show it in different ways – especially as I lack self-confidence and often have doubts in my head that are not based in reality. There is a fine line though, I couldn't spend much time with someone who was 'soppy' all the time. I do like a man to be a man most of the time, but just to show his soft side to me from time to time, in little ways that I understand.

9. How do you feel about physical contact in a relationship?

If we're talking sexual contact with the man I love then I'm mostly all for it. There are some days though when I'm in a particularly childish mood when I am unable to make the transition into an adult again, and it just feels strange. With regard to non-sexual contact, I prefer any contact to be firm – for example a strong deep hug or a massage offers a lot more pleasure than being lightly stroked, which makes me go really twitchy and want to break free. I don't like holding hands when walking as it irritates me, I

74

think it somehow interferes with my ability to walk normally, it seems to set me off balance.

10. Do you feel comfortable with emotional interaction?

Assuming this question refers to verbal discussion of emotions there are two parts to my answer. If my husband and I are sharing emotions about each other then I'm absolutely fine with it as I have plenty of first-hand experience to draw on. Talking about our feelings is important as I seem unable to simply 'pick up on them' which could otherwise leave me with many unnerving blanks. However, if my husband wants to talk about his emotions towards something else – music, for example – I often find it very difficult to interact, as his feelings and experiences are so different to my own and the whole discussion quickly takes on a very metaphysical form which my head tunes out from involuntarily. I wish that I could share his passions and enthusiasm for things that are important to him, but I simply do not know how to make my brain engage in these kind of discussions. I have tried, but it only results in what seems to me to be no more than meaningless rambling.

I think in general I can only interact if I have previous direct personal experience of the emotion in hand. I can fully understand and empathize with somebody's feelings when a pet dies, for example, as I have been through this many times and am aware of the feelings that come with it.

Strangely I feel more able to relate to other people's negative emotions as opposed to positive ones but I think there are more 'rules' with regard to how negative emotions should be dealt with. What I mean is, people tend to be serious when they feel negative and people are generally more logical when being serious, which helps me to understand what they are saying.

11. Do you hope to marry or have a long-term relationship?

I am in a very happy (if volatile) marriage wherein we both make a real effort to accept each other's strengths and weaknesses. I have always sought a long- term meaningful relationship since I was in my teens.

12. Would you like to have a family?

I really don't know. If you had asked me this question a couple of years ago the answer would have been a definite 'no'. I have no maternal instinct whatsoever and am not sure that this will ever change. Sometimes I like the idea of having a family, but I find it extremely difficult to interact with babies and young children as they are so loud and silly and make me feel very awkward and dull and monotone. Combine this with the fact that I am

self-centred and can yet barely take care of myself with regard to domestic duties, I am not sure that I am parent material.

13. Do you feel that a relationship with someone else with AS or a similar personality would be preferable?

I don't think being AS or NT is relevant as everyone is an individual no matter if they have a neurological label or not. I'm sure there are both Aspies and NTs that I could get on with really well just as there are Aspies and NTs in the world that would wind me up beyond belief. I have no experience of an AS-AS relationship so I cannot make a comparison.

14. Do you feel pressure to be in a relationship by society?

Not at all. I have always taken great pride in making my own choices, particularly ones that are in conflict with the ideas of society!

15. Do you feel you have sufficient empathy to have a relationship?

Well, I have managed to maintain several relationships with hardly any empathy, but I think I would have had a smoother ride over the years had I been more able to understand my partners' thoughts and feelings. A part of my diagnosis included scoring my EQ (Empathy Quotient) and it wasn't a huge surprise to find out I only got 8 out of 80. More than one past boyfriend had told me that it upset them that I never thought to ask them how they felt or how their day had been. I wasn't being rude, things like that simply never enter my mind.

Useful Contacts

The Missing Link Support Services Ltd.

For Individuals

Counselling, Psychotherapy, Social Skills, Specific Individual Support, Diagnosis, Employment Support, Training, Social Group, Social Support and Assessment

For Professionals

Training, Consultation and Workshops

For Carers

Training, Consultation, Counselling and Individual Support

Contact

www.missinglinksupportservice.co.uk

Telephone: 07971 569042

Email: vicky@missinglinksupportservice.co.uk

genevieve@missinglinksupportservice.co.uk

Asperger's syndrome websites

Discussion Forums, Chat rooms, Real life meet-ups for AS adults in the UK and Ireland

Aspietalk and Aspie Village

www.aspietalk.co.uk

www.aspievillage.org.uk

The Asperger Personal Guide

Rasing Self-Esteem and Making the Most of Yourself as an Adult with Asperger's Syndrome

Genevieve Edmonds and Dean Worton

Following on from the **Asperger Love Guide** and **Social Guide**, this third book in the series of self-help practical life guides aims to cover the personal issues that an adult with Asperger's syndrome faces in a world not designed for people with autism.

Written from a male and female perspective of two Asperger's adults, it looks at:

- the positive aspects of Asperger's syndrome
- how these translate into everyday life
- whether Asperger's syndrome is in fact a disability
- strategies to gain mental and physical health as an adult with Asperger's syndrome

The book aims to help adults gain self-esteem and get the most out of themselves as a unique adult with Asperger's syndrome. These courageous authors have drawn upon their personal experiences to provide an outstanding series of books aimed at supporting and enhancing the quality of life for other Asperger adults.

Genevieve Edmonds is a 23 year old with 'residual' Asperger's syndrome, which she views as a significant gift. She works as an associate of the Missing Link Support Service in Lancashire supporting individuals with ASD. She speaks and writes frequently in the field of Autism, along with giving training, workshops and counselling, and aims to empower those with ASD, carers and professionals in the understanding of Asperger's syndrome as a difference rather than an impairment.

Dean Worton is a 31 year old high functioning individual with a very positive expression of Asperger's syndrome. He runs a successful UK-based website for adults with Asperger's syndrome, and hosts real-life meet-ups around the UK for its members. His key interest is in encouraging adults to live positively and successfully with the gifts that Asperger's syndrome provides.

Lucky Duck Books
October 2006 - 128 pages Paperback (978-1-4129-2257-9)

Order online at www.PaulChapmanPublishing.co.uk

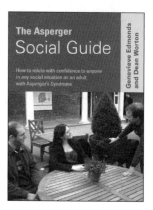